**Books by Rosemary Rosedale**

My Dog Munye
Munye Matters

# MUNYE MATTERS
## A TRUE STORY

Rosemary Rosedale

Munye Matters

Rosemary Rosedale

© 2025 Cosmos Press

ISBN 978-0-9935332-8-0

The right of the author to be identified as the author of this work has been asserted in accordance with the Copyright, Designs and Patents Act 1988.

Photography copyright the author

All rights reserved.

No part of this publication may be reproduced, stored in a retrieval system, or transmitted, in any form or by any means, electronic, mechanical, photocopying, recording or otherwise, without the prior permission of the copyright owners.

**COSMOS PRESS**

*For Aiden*

*Dotty about dogs*

# Contents

Munye is Miserable                    9

Brothers and Sisters for Munye        17

Terrible Trauma                       25

Then there were Two                   33

The Survivor                          39

Happiness is...                       47

A Burst Bubble                        53

Christmas                             59

Munye and Friends                     65

About King Charles Spaniels           66

# Munye is Miserable

It mattered to me that my dog was so miserable. Munye wasn't his friendly, mischievous self. Instead of wagging his tail when he saw me he just stood and looked with big mournful eyes, tail drooping between his legs. All the bounce had gone out of him.

He disappeared for long periods. Sometimes I found him alone at the bottom of the garden moping, or curled up asleep. He was sleeping more than usual and looked droopy and unhappy. Why?

"Danny." Mum's voice invaded my thoughts. "Won't you take Munye for a walk? He hasn't been out all day." *That's a good idea*, I thought. I felt like going out, so for once I didn't argue that it was my brother's turn!

"All right Mum," I called back. "I'll take him."

Nothing is straightforward! I searched for Munye's harness for 10 minutes before finding it on the dining room floor. Phew!

Munye actually showed signs of excitement.

Usually, whenever we mention the magic words 'walk' or 'walkies', he goes wild, spinning round and round at a great rate of turns. In between he jumps up on his hind legs and, still turning, lets out yelps of delight. He isn't still for a millisecond. It makes it really hard to clip the lead onto his harness. On that day it was easy.

At last we were on our way! Once we got going he cheered up though he still wasn't himself until we'd left the traffic behind and reached the open fields.

Munye swiftly and fearlessly sized up every dog in sight. The bigger the dog the bolder he became.

The best dog he met that day was a Border collie. They took their time sniffing each other out.

*Hello! You're so tiny!*

They obviously liked each other

*Yes! But I'm black and white and I'm fast! Let's run!*

and raced off together around the field.

Guess what? Munye kept up with Collie!

"All things have an end, except a sausage. It has two!" (That is what my Norwegian great-grandmother used to say, so I am told.) Unfortunately my walk with Munye had an end. It was time to go home. As soon I clipped his lead onto his harness his mood changed. Instead of darting here and there exploring and sniffing at everything, he walked limply beside me tail drooping.

When we got home he slumped. He was visibly sorry for himself. His cage looked cold and uninviting.

Not even Miss Piggy or Pengu managed to draw him into it.

We took turns to distract him.

*Nobody understands me. Nothing is the same without Mamma around. But I know she is upstairs!* **Why** *can't I see her?*

I climbed inside the cage. Munye followed. I cuddled him, and tried to play, but he remained sad and listless.

After a while I got cramp so I climbed out. Munye followed but went outside.

Later I went out to see what Munye was doing. What a funny sight I saw.

Zulu was doing acrobatics on the lawn. She rolled over and over and seemed to be grinning at Munye. For once he did not try to chase Zulu but sat a little distance away from her staring solemnly at her antics. When Munye tired of that he droopily went inside.

My brother, Aiden, tried to amuse him but Munye wasn't interested. Aiden gave up and tucked himself up on the sofa to read a book. Munye was soon snoring next to him.

At the end of the day we found Munye snuggled up to Ntombi happier, but still sad. You could see she was listening to Munye - really listening with both ears. I thought I overheard this:

*You do understand, don't you Ntombi?*

*Purr-rr, I do, Munye. But let me tell you my story...*

*"When I was 6 weeks old I was taken away from my mother. It was scary. My 5 brothers and sisters and I were moved far from home and kept in a cramped cage. It was noisy. Dogs barked and whined, cats meowed and called day and night.*

*But in some ways it was better ...*

*When we were all together at home with mother we heard terrible rows between 'him and her'. These would always end with the threat of drowning all of us kittens! Mother kept calm and kept us close until the worst day of my life happened. They dragged us from her. Ugh! Can't talk about it...*

*I still miss my Mother terribly. She was ...the best."*

With that Ntombi sat up straight and, looking down on Munye, continued.

Lecture over, the cat and dog friends fell sleep - exhausted.

# Brothers and Sisters for Munye

MEANWHILE UPSTAIRS THINGS had been happening!

It all began early on Saturday morning two days before the puppies were due. Mum was in the bathroom cleaning Sawubona (Sabbie for short) and cutting the hair underneath her belly. This is done so that the puppies are able to suckle more easily.

Suddenly Mum got a surprise! Two little legs were sticking out of Sabbie's birth canal. This is dangerous. You see, like a human, a puppy should be born headfirst. If the feet come out first (called a breach birth) it takes longer for the puppy to be born. If it doesn't breathe oxygen in time it may die or be damaged for life.

Mum knew what she had to do. She took hold of the little legs and when Sabbie gave a push, Mum pulled gently. Out came a stunning Tri-colour 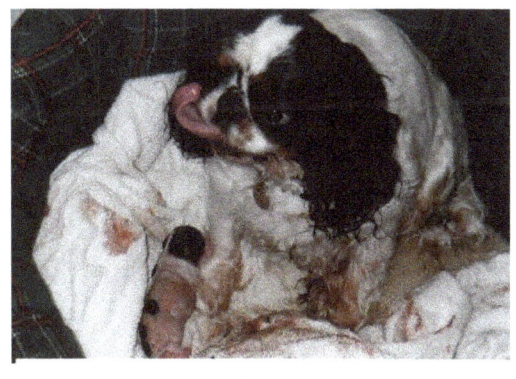 puppy. It was the first puppy to be born on the bathroom floor! It started to cry straight away – a good sign, as it means the puppy is alive and well.

Sabbie got busy licking her puppy clean with her long tongue. I hadn't realised how slimy newborn puppies are! Birth sure is a bloody and messy business! But Sabbie took control and soon the puppy was shiny white and pitch black!

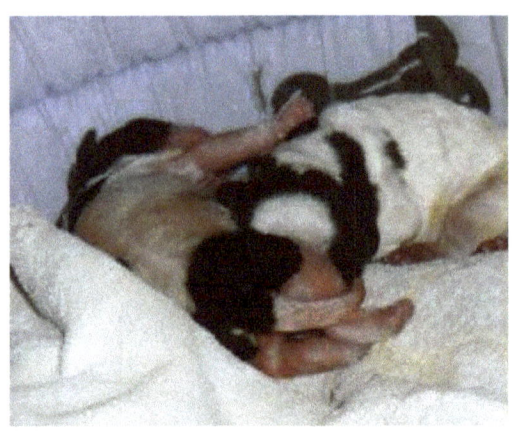

Soon Sabbie got restless and quickly the next puppy arrived.

The first puppy, a female, had already been named Zuma. (Zuma is Zulu meaning 'Surprise'). Zuma snuggled up and welcomed her slimy brother. She didn't seem to mind the slime!

Spot the difference!

My brother told me all this. You see, he was allowed to be in on the birth and I wasn't. I wasn't happy. Didn't think that was fair. Mum explained I was needed to look after my dog Munye! I thought this was just an excuse. But Munye was very unhappy, as I have already told you. One thing I had to do was make sure he didn't manage to go upstairs.

Mum said she really needed a helper and that

Aiden was calm and knew what to do. He seemed to like doing this!

Aiden came downstairs for a drink and told me there were two puppies. I tried to tell Munye. I am not sure he understood.

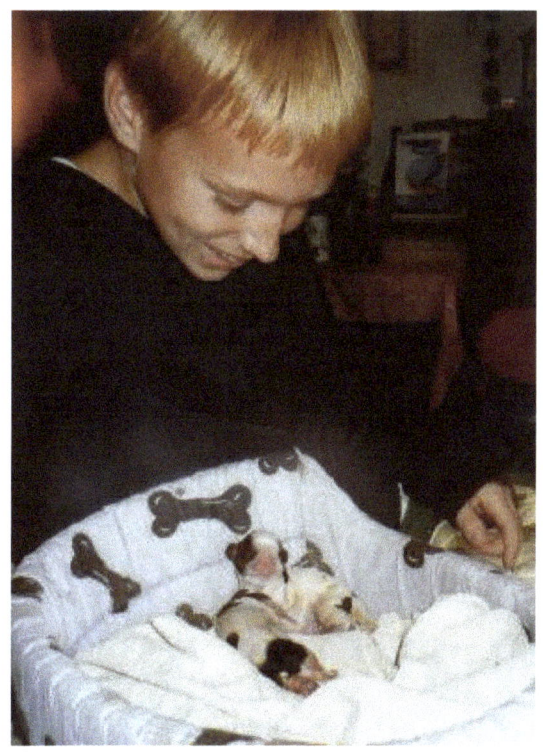

It was weeks later that I saw this picture of Aiden with the first two puppies. I couldn't help thinking I had missed out on something.

Aiden never let me forget that he was the one who helped deliver the puppies.

I reminded him that I had my dog Munye. And it was unlikely that Dad would let him keep a puppy.

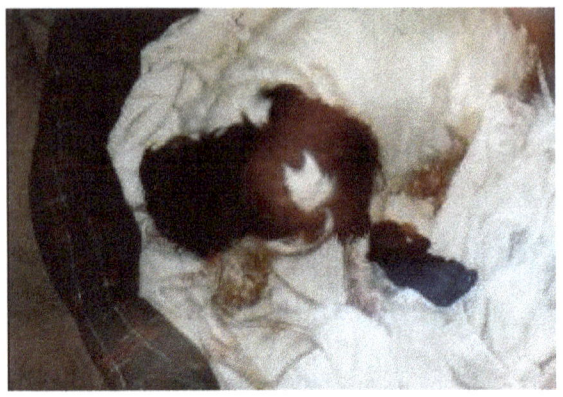

Sawubona was kept very busy. She had hardly finished cleaning Little-boy-two when number three arrived – a black surprise!

Sabbie stared at him strangely through the weird blue glow surrounding him. He was different.

I suspect Sabbie was thinking he looked like his Black and Tan father!

His brother and sister, who had been minded by Aiden, were brought back to join Sabbie and the new puppy.

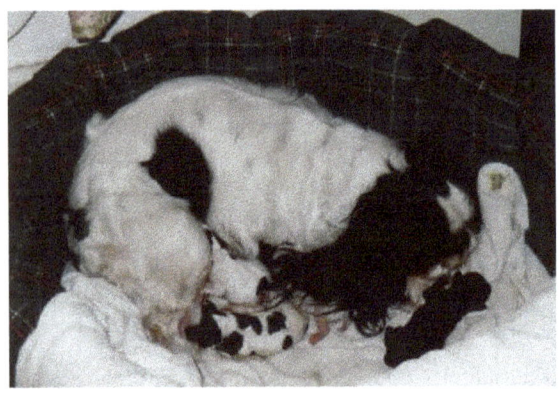

They all snuggled up and began to search for milk.

Sabbie fell asleep for a bit! When she woke she started cleaning herself again with her long tongue.

Having puppies seems like hard work!

Aiden was watching closely when to his surprise he spotted a fourth puppy. She had slid silently into this world with even her mother hardly noticing. Can you spot Number-Four in the previous picture?

When all the cleaning was over all four puppies snuggled close to Sabbie and latched on for a good feed. She seemed most content.

Four puppies – phew! Now my work is cut out ... And there is Munye too. I do love all my babies!

On the day after they were born, I was allowed into the puppy-nursery to help choose their names. As is our tradition we called them Zulu names. We looked at each one very carefully and thought of a suitable name. Here is the line-up giving their Zulu names, the English translation, weight at birth and the birth-order, starting from the left.

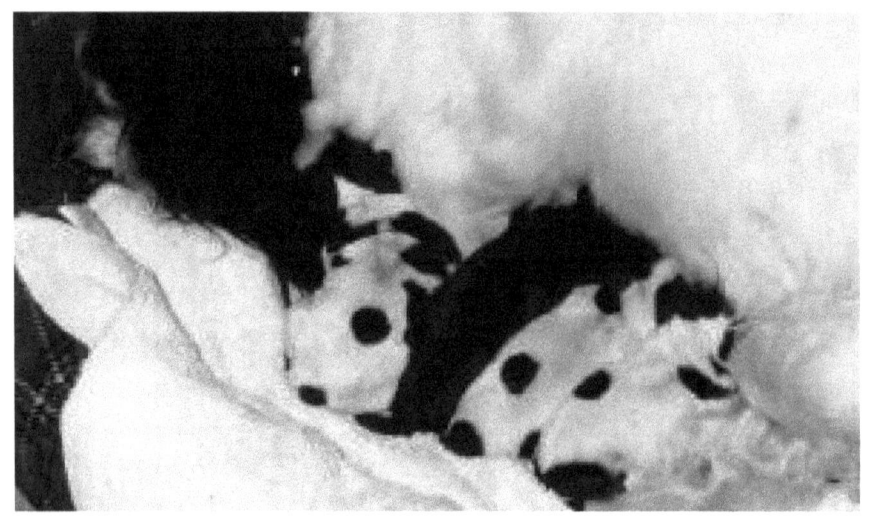

[1] *Zuma* (Surprise)
   180 g, born 09.00
   Tri-colour girl, (left)

[3] *Jabula* (Happiness)
   135 g, born 10.06
   Black and Tan boy, (second left)

[4] *Ibala* (Spot)
   120 g, born, 11.24
   Tiny tri-colour girl, (second right)

[2] *Phila* (Survivor)
   145 g born 09.30
   Tri-colour boy (right)

Phila was special to Aiden. You see, when Phila was born he was lifeless. Mum held him upside down to drain his lungs. Then she cradled him in her left hand and rubbed him with her right. After what seemed forever he made a little rasping sound. Aiden and Mum cheered! Then Aiden took over until Phila was breathing normally. It was so good to have four living puppies.

# Terrible Trauma

SABBIE WAS CONTENT. Except for quick trips out for necessary business she spent all her time in her basket with her four new babies. Licking, feeding and cleaning up after them, washing herself, sleeping and eating took up all her time.

The puppies slept, fed, or moved around in search of food. They had surprisingly loud squeaky voices and made a real racket whenever they couldn't find what they were looking for.

This worried Sabbie until she found the 'squeaker' and pawed the stray puppy back into the range of milk. After getting a lick all over it settled down to suckle.

During the puppies' first two days I hardly saw my mother or brother. They were so busy minding the puppies, checking the electric blanket was working, feeding Sabbie and watching the new babies.

Every so often Mum and Aiden got a fright as one of the puppies seemed to be missing. After a search they would find it under Sabbie's ear or tail.

*I didn't know puppies were so exhausting. I need sleep*

Sometimes Sabbie was found lying on top of one! Aiden would rescue the puppy and tell Sabbie off. Clearly Sabbie was very tired and didn't realise she was smothering the puppy. So, Aiden forgave her.

How puppies survive at all I do not know!

Downstairs Munye remained miserable. I kept on trying to play with him but he wasn't interested. He spent a lot of time sleeping. Whenever he was awake he tried desperately to get upstairs. When he managed to get into Mum and Dad's bedroom, where his mother and the puppies were, he was immediately scolded and sent back downstairs. It was sad! I also felt left out and sorry for myself. I was hardly ever allowed to stay with the new puppies. Mum said I was too boisterous.

On the evening of the second day Mum said she thought Sabbie looked off colour. Dad said not to fuss. Neither of them slept much as pups kept squeaking all night. Mum and Dad took it in turns to get up and see what was going on. They usually found a puppy lost at the very edge of the basket and put it back to suck. Sabbie wasn't interested.

Early that morning the puppy's cries became desperate.

*I feel ghastly!*

*I don't want my puppies near me. Strange! I so badly wanted them and now I wish they would all go away.*

*I'm so tired. Perhaps I'm ill.*

Mum found Sabbie lying on the floor and the puppies alone. It is vital for puppies to drink and be warm if they are to survive. For the next few hours Mum and Dad worked to hard trying to get Sabbie to stay with her pups. But it didn't work.

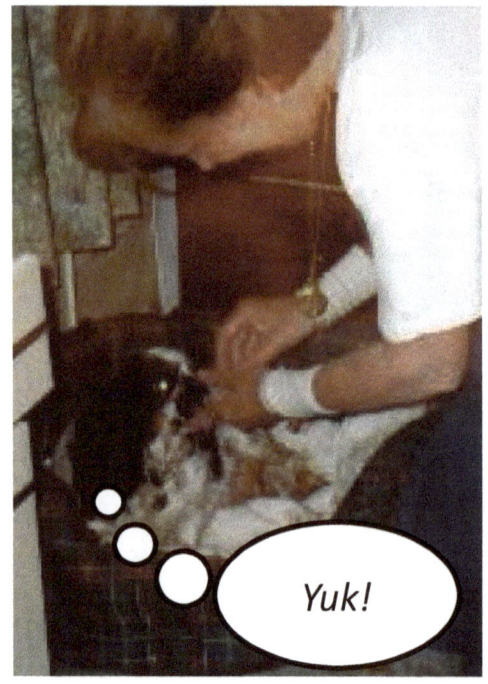

By morning it was obvious that Sabbie was very sick. She had a high temperature and there was a horrid smell coming from her basket. Most worrying she was ignoring her puppies.

Mum and Aiden rushed all of them to the vet.

Sabbie had an infection the vet said, and injected her with an antibiotic. He gave Mum liquid antibiotic to give her everyday. Sabbie really didn't like this but Mum made sure she took it.

Sabbie soon seemed to be getting better but the puppies were looking fragile. They seemed to find it difficult to suck.

Mum talked it over with her friend, Joyce who owns Boy-Blue, the puppies' father. Joyce said they must be kept in a cage to stop Sabbie abandoning them. Sabbie hated being caged and often tried to escape. At least the puppies could feed.

On the third day, real tragedy struck. Phila, who had been stillborn and then revived, stopped trying to suck. Suddenly Aiden noticed she had stopped breathing. He remembered how Mum had revived him at birth. He picked Phila up and started rubbing him firmly. To his amazement, after about 10 minutes, Phila was breathing again. Sadly life did not last for long for Phila. In just over an hour he died. Aiden was really upset and so was Mum.

Phila was a game little puppy but he wasn't strong enough to survive Sabbie's fever.

Aiden gave Phila to me. As I looked at him I remembered Munye's older brother. We decided to bury Phila under the red tree next to his Big Brother.

Then they were three: **Zuma, Jabula, Ibala.**

The puppies seemed strong though Jabula was a bit floppy. Aiden liked Jabula, the Black and Tan, the most. He had a cute little white nail-shaped stripe on his head. He seemed a happy fellow and lived up to his name – Happiness.

The puppies slept in such funny positions. When alone they huddled and piled up. That night the puppies were noisy. Mum and Dad did not sleep.

On the morning of the fourth day, Mum and Aiden noticed the Jabula was looking weaker. He had lost weight and was not feeding. Aiden watched him like a hawk and tried to encourage him to latch on to his Mamma and suck. When this didn't work Mum mixed up dilute Carnation milk and tried to feed Jabula using a tiny bottle. He drank a little but a while later Aiden found him dead. No amount of rubbing revived him.

We were all very upset, especially Aiden. He just handed over Jabula in a piece of paper and said he wasn't coming with me to bury him. So I had to bury Jabula by myself.

No one was looking as I laid him in a grave next to his two older brothers. A tear trickled down my cheek as the little bundle disappeared under a spade-full of soil.

I had lots of questions. How come I was burying a puppy for the third time? Why did they die when they were so young and cute?

I had no answers.

I walked droopily back to the house. There a sad Munye waited for me. Did he realise what had happened? In a flash I realised how glad I was that he was alive and well and decided from that moment I was going to be a better Munye-owner! We had rough and tumble and a lot of fun. Munye seemed to be getting his smile back.

# Then there were Two

IT WAS THE fourth day since the puppies were born. Why had both boys died while the girls were still alive? Joyce told us it was a fact that male puppies were weaker. I asked myself whether it is the same with human babies. I had no answer!

Here are the two.

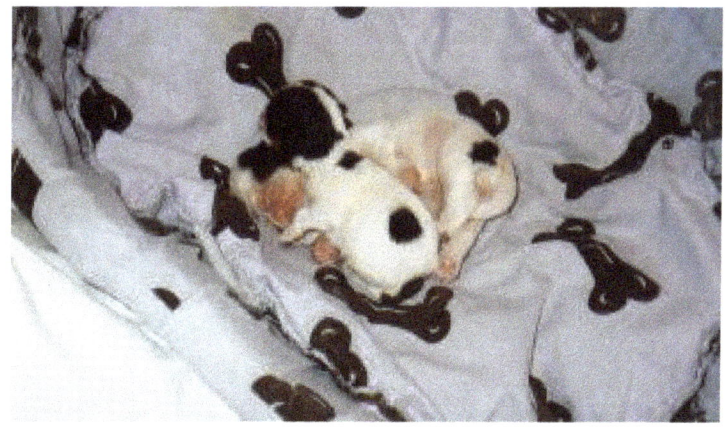

**Zuma**, the first-born, is the one on top. The other is **Ibala**, the youngest and smallest of the puppies who we renamed **Phila-II** after her dead brother.

By then we were all really worried. We wondered whether these two would live. Aiden and Mum watched them very closely. They weighed the puppies every day. Soon we noticed a big change in Zuma who was always sucking vigorously, and Phila who didn't seem that interested in food. When

Zuma was born she weighed 180 grams and went down to 155 grams. (Puppies almost always lose weight after they are born.) On the tenth day Zuma weighed 300 grams but little Phila, 120 grams at birth, had gained only 20 grams weighed 140 grams.

Sawubona noticed the difference.

One day Phila was missing. On looking closely Aiden found her buried under the towels Sabbie had 'dug' up. Sabbie was always keen on digging.

Mum and Aiden took Sawubona and puppies back to the vet. He dosed them with antibiotics and said Phila must be fed on special puppy milk every two hours day and night.

Mum started Phila's feeds straight away. Phila spluttered at every meal. Mum was bothered. Was she using the feeding bottle properly?

Then Dad had a go. He insisted on feeding Phila in the dining room. So, at last Munye saw one of his sisters but he looked away, I think he didn't like the bottle!

Dad was an instant expert. No more spluttering. He became chief feeder. Phila didn't get any bigger. Zuma did. I thought Zuma might pop!

It as just was well Dad took over the feeding as Mum

had to go away for ten days. Dad did really well. He let me hold little Phila sometimes. I couldn't believe how small she was.

At last! Phila began to gain weight. Hurrah! She went up from 140 grams to 160 grams. But Dad was losing weight, he said. He had to get up at least twice every night to feed Phila, do all the shopping and cooking for us, and all the rest. We tried to help with the chores but it wasn't easy to remember. Poor old Dad!

Two mornings before Mum came home we found Phila in a very bad state. She had lost weight and looked like a starved rat. Zuma tried to keep her warm. Sabbie looked alarmed. It was no use. It was time for Phila to die.

Dad looked so sad. He had grown fond of her and tried to help Phila live. He kept saying over and over again: "Poor little bugger! Poor little bugger!"

As you might guess I had to bury Phila. Perhaps I'll become an undertaker!

# The Survivor

ZUMA SURVIVED. ZUMA was strong and daring. Zuma would definitely go far in life. You only had to look at her to know deep thoughts of mischief and adventure were whirling in her brain. She was always planning her next move.

When the other puppies were alive we thought Zuma seemed greedy. She would push them out of the way and take over their feeding spot. Mum and Aiden did not like this.

I came to realise that Zuma had survived because of her self-preserving qualities. I was so glad she lived especially when I was allowed to play with her.

One day Joyce came to visit. I thought I saw Zuma

wink at her.

Joyce thought Zuma was rather special and may even be a show dog when she was older.

Joyce said she might be interested in buying her. I did not like the idea of parting with Zuma. Aiden wanted her as his own puppy.

About this time I heard Zuma talking to Sabbie.

*I want to get out of here and run!*

*You must learn to walk first, young lady!*

Zuma looked afraid and didn't budge.

Munye had been waiting his chance. When he thought no one was looking he sneaked into the puppy-room and said his first proper hello to his little sister. He did not seem to realise that we were in there too and watching him.

This gave Zuma courage.

Funny, sometimes brothers and sisters are the best teachers.

She kept her eyes fixed on Munye as he moved away then flopped out of her basket after him. The next thing we saw was Zuma heading off to inspect the family tree.

*Who are these people*

*That must be my Mamma when she was a puppy.*

*What fun!*

Zuma suddenly spied Munye and Sabbie in the big basket. She waddled off to join them. There wasn't much room but it was very snug, very snug indeed. She squeezed in between them.

Sabbie was snoring loudly, as always!

Munye had his eyes open but seemed asleep. He looked as though

*This is the life!*

he had reached heaven! For Zuma this was a first.

Like Munye at that age, Zuma was soon into everything. It seemed there was nothing she would not try. One day I caught her trying to open the French door leading to the conservatory!

Zuma was most observant!

After a long and valiant try at opening with absolutely no success, Zuma spotted Ntombi. (They had made friends before). Zuma did not like to admit defeat so pretended that Ntombi was more important than her door-opening project and ran towards her.

At that point Dad wandered in, cup of tea in hand. Soon all three were on the pink chair.

*Take it easy Zuma! There is plenty of time to learn about opening doors!*

Ntombi was interested in everyone and was often found listening or telling people what to do. But she could also be a bully. She did not like her sister Zulu much and often duffed her up.

Zulu was shy but loved little Zuma. After all they were the only ones whose names began with a Z!

*You snuggle up to me Zuma. We'll have some fun.*

Zuma was such a tiger! Everyone wanted a turn to be with her.

Aiden was working on Dad to keep Zuma. I didn't think he stood a chance but usually managed to keep my mouth shut.

Later I found Zuma having a confidential chat with Ntombi. I knew it must be secret stuff as they kept quiet when they saw me. I didn't catch what they were saying but for once Zuma looked serious. It had definitely got her thinking.

At the end of the day I found Zuma alone. She was asleep and was holding a toothbrush! She opened one eye and winked.

Amazing!

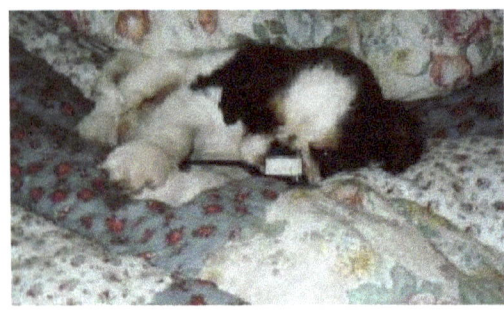

Have you ever heard of the puppy who wants to brush her teeth - without even being told to do so?

# Happiness is...

MUNYE HAD NEVER been happier. He was totally dotty over his little sister Zuma. She was such good fun. They spent every possible minute together either playing or sleeping.

*Happiness is ...*

having a sister who is energetic and likes to play.

Munye loved to tease Zuma. On this occasion he raided the kitchen and found a carrot.

*Have this, Zuma*

*Come on then, get it!*

Munye ran to Zuma and offered it to her. As soon as she took it the tug-of-war began! They kept the family in fits of laughter.

"This is better entertainment than TV!" said Dad.

Zuma ran away and hid when she'd had enough.

Before long she went in search of her Mamma. I'm sure she wanted to tell her about the carrot. She also wanted a drink! Happiness is... feeding your baby.

Munye got the nickname 'Jealous-Bags'. He couldn't bear to see his Mamma paying attention to anyone else – not even to his sister. He always wants to be the centre of attention but does not always get his own way!

When they were all tired they joined Miss Piggy in the basket. She was a faithful friend. Miss Piggy was always there when any of the animals needed her – even if they flattened her!

*Happiness is* ... having a true friend.

The first time Zuma was allowed into the garden her Mamma and Munye carefully escorted her. He eyes were wide open and her nose was

> *I smell with my little nose something beginning with B!*
>
> *And, I am going to find it!*

sniffing overtime. There were so many bright colours and interesting shapes and smells.

Munye loved pointing out his favourites and that "happiness is ...' exploring the garden.

Zuma decided to explore alone.

Zuma became confident outside very quickly. She loved to tear off down the garden path and round the corner to the back gate. When she realised she couldn't open the gate she spun round and raced all the way back. This became a game. There is no doubt about it she is an outdoor girl.

Happiness is lots of things. It can be discovering who you are!

"Is there such a thing as lasting happiness?" I wondered.

*See the pretty girl in that mirror there ...*

*Woops! I think it might be me.*

Mum says happiness is sometimes like a beautiful bubble blown out of a bubble-pipe. One millisecond there is nothing there. In the next a bubble grows out of the pipe, until it breaks free and floats away, rainbow coloured in the air. Surprise and delight are yours. You see it, chase it, and catch it! It bursts! Even if you do not catch it, it has a short life cycle of its own.

And so it was with Munye's Zuma-bubble. He was so happy and couldn't imagine life without Zuma. But, suddenly she was gone.

# A Burst Bubble

MUM WAS PLAYING with Zuma on her lap when the phone rang. "Hello Joyce" she said. They talked for quite a while. "That will be fine. Zuma will be bathed and ready for you by ten tomorrow morning." Zuma pricked up her ears when she heard her name. Her worst fears were coming true.

It took a while to sink in. When Zuma realised the time had come for her leave home, and go somewhere new, she was devastated. She liked Joyce a lot but could not bear the thought of leaving her Mamma and Munye, and the two-legged friends she had known all her life. What could she do?

*Sam, I have to leave tomorrow. I don't want to. Can you help?*

Zuma had to confide in someone quickly. She spied Sam the Stone Snail and poured out her misery to him. Sam was a very good listener but said nothing.

Zuma then searched for Munye and told him the bad news. Munye was so shocked he couldn't say anything. He turned his back on Zuma and she was left to grieve alone.

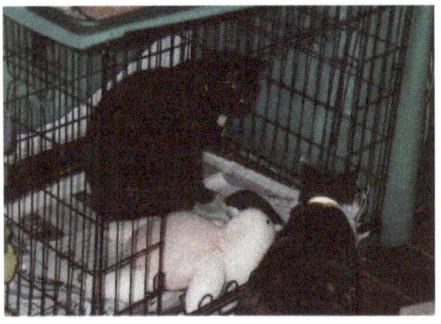

Zulu and Ntombi overheard the news and went and told Miss Piggy.

*Oh boneless and wise Miss Piggy, I can't bear this. Three of my babies died. Now my little Zuma-zoom is also going.*

*I'm so sorry Sabbie.*

*Be strong. You must think of Munye.*

She was bowled over with disbelief and anguish. The cats sat with her for a long time trying to cheer her up. Then they left to curl up and sleep.

Sawubona was the last to find out. When Zuma told her she was overcome with sadness. She dragged herself off to see the best comforter she knew - Miss Piggy.

It was Aiden who managed comfort Zuma.

*Cheer up Zuma. You are going to a lovely home. Joyce will look after you. And, you will live with your Pappa. There are lots of other dogs for you to play with too.*

*I'll come and visit - promise!*

*Think of it as an adventure.*

*I'll try. Promise!*

So Zuma left on a positive note.

I took the dogs for a walk when Joyce came for Zuma. When we got back Munye didn't notice Zuma wasn't there. He was very interested in the cheese-roll he had just found.

Sabbie could not resist the challenge. It wasn't long before she had stolen and hidden the prize. At first Munye couldn't work out where it had gone.

He was suspicious and walked up to where his mother was sitting.

What could he smell? Cheese!

Eventually Sabbie gave in! She knew just how far to push Munye.

# Christmas

I turned over, stretched, yawned and opened my eyes. It was strangely quiet. My first thought was "Two days till Christmas. What will I get?" I tiptoed into my parents' room. They were having a cup of tea. "Open the curtains Danny," said Dad.

Daylight hit my eyes. "WOW!" I yelled full volume, "SNOW". My wish had come true. We would have a white Christmas.

I rushed downstairs. All the animals were on the settee in the lounge in front of the coal fire. Ntombi was the first to wake up.

"Come on Munye," I yelled, "let's play in the snow". He did not need a second invitation. I made snowballs and drew in the snow. Munye explored, sniffing every bit of the garden. Then I remembered Aiden! I ran upstairs and woke him. Soon we were having a snowball fight and waking up the neighbourhood!

Munye had tried to make the most of things but there was no denying he missed Zuma very much. Mum says it is normal to miss those you love even more at happy times like Christmas.

After breakfast we had fun putting up the decorations. Our manger is in a Zulu hut resting on a bead-mat. The figures of baby Jesus, Mary and Joseph, the ass and the ox, came from Rome.

"Christmas should be a time to give, not just a time to get," said Mum. "It is about happiness that lasts - a mystery tied up with this little Baby".

"Is this true?" I pondered. "I want to be happy - everyone does."

*Exciting white stuff!*

*Mamma won't play. Wish Zuma were here.*

Talking about happiness, Sawubona did not look too happy. I heard Munye name-calling her. Sabbie remained dignified.

Munye was sorry and said so.

Dad picked up Munye and his mother. Ntombi, not one to be left out, jumped up too.

Mum moved over and gave them each a cuddle.

Christmas was special that year. Loads of getting and giving! It was good to be together even if little Zuma-zoom wasn't with us.

*Ha! Ha!*
*Fatty-chops. You've got a double chin*

*I hear you, Munye!*
*Why don't you try to make someone happy this Christmas instead of wasting time trying to bully me?*

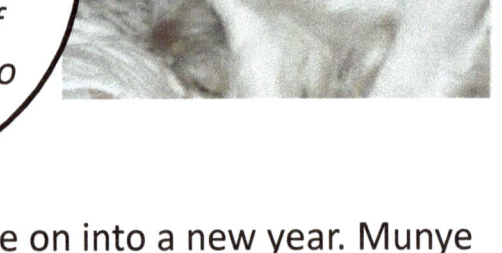

The time came to move on into a new year. Munye and I had great fun destroying old things!

"What will the future hold?" I wondered. There will be lots more to tell about Munye of that I am sure.

# Munye and Friends

## Their names and meanings

**Zulu** is a language (with lots of clicks) spoken by the **Zulu people** who mainly live in South Africa. Our animals all have Zulu names.

### Zulu

A Zulu coloured cat – a tortoiseshell female. Zulu, born in 1997, has a soft, silent walk and very soft purr. She was mine but now she belongs to Dad.

### Ntombi

A tortoiseshell female cat that wears a large white bib! She is Zulu's twin sister, born in 1997. Ntombi means "girl". Ntombi walks noisily, purrs loudly, and belongs to my brother. These two are 'alley-cats'.

### Sawubona

A pedigree King Charles spaniel. Sawubona means "Hello" said in a friendly way. Sawubona is shy and loyal to all the family. She was born in January 1997 and was our first pet. Sabbie belongs to Mum.

### Munye

A pedigree King Charles spaniel. Munye means "One" - the only pup from Sawubona's first litter. Born in 1999, he is intelligent, energetic, and excitable (like me). He likes everyone and is the best dog in the whole world. Munye is mine.

## Sawubona's second litter

**Phila** (Survivor) Tri-colour boy.      Born 2-09-00 died 4-09-00
**Jabula** (Happiness) Black-and-Tan boy.      Born 2-09-00 died 5-09-00
**Ibala** (Spot) Tri-colour girl.      Born 2-09-00 died 2-10-00
**Zuma** (Surprise) Tri-colour girl.      Born 2-09-00 very much alive!

## About King Charles Spaniels

Mystery! Nobody knows exactly when the King Charles Spaniel breed was started. But, the first written reference to the breed in England is around 1570.

There are some funny stories.

Queen Elizabeth I called these little dogs 'Comforters' or 'Gentle Spaniels'. Ladies of The Court kept them under their voluminous skirts close to the feet and body! In 1587 someone wrote that a tiny blood soaked spaniel was found under the skirts of Mary Queen of Scots, after she was executed. It was taken away and washed. During the reigns of King Charles I and King Charles II, from 1625 to 1685, these little dogs became very popular. King Charles II named them after himself. His palace was full of them and the King was often seen walking in St. James' park followed by several of his dogs. Today, given half a chance, Charlies (their nickname) will dive under bedclothes, snuggle close to the occupant, and start snoring!

**Charlies come in four colours.**

**Black and Tan** (glossy black with mahogany and tan markings)

**Tricolour** (pearly white with black patches) and bright tan markings on cheeks, above eyes etc.)

**Blenheim** (white with chestnut-red patches)

**Ruby** (a rich chestnut-red 'whole colour').

Adults weigh 6 to 12 pounds (about 2.7 to 5.4 Kgs.). Charlies have a large domed head, a stubby black nose, long ears and the most beautiful large, sad and expressive eyes. They are gentle, fun loving, loyal, friendly and don't bite or bark very much! They keep themselves clean.

Sadly some end up in rescue homes when their owners die or don't want them.

**Do you?**

If you want to know more read:

The King Charles Spaniel;
by M. Joyce Birchall 1987;
ISBN 0707106125

www.ingramcontent.com/pod-product-compliance
Lightning Source LLC
Chambersburg PA
CBHW042301030526
44119CB00066B/839